David Smith Coddington

Eulogy on President Lincoln

David Smith Coddington

Eulogy on President Lincoln

ISBN/EAN: 9783743326354

Manufactured in Europe, USA, Canada, Australia, Japa

Cover: Foto ©ninafisch / pixelio.de

Manufactured and distributed by brebook publishing software
(www.brebook.com)

David Smith Coddington

Eulogy on President Lincoln

EULOGY

ON

PRESIDENT LINCOLN,

BY

DAVID S. CODDINGTON,

DELIVERED IN THE

CITADEL SQUARE CHURCH, CHARLESTON, S. C.,

May 6th, 1865,

AT THE REQUEST OF THE OFFICERS AND SOLDIERS IN THE
NORTHERN DISTRICT, DEPARTMENT OF THE SOUTH.

He is dead yet speaketh.

NEW YORK:
BAKER & GODWIN, PRINTERS,
PRINTING-HOUSE SQUARE.
1865.

HEADQUARTERS NORTHERN DISTRICT,
DEPARTMENT OF THE SOUTH,
CHARLESTON, S. C., April 20, 1865.

Hon. D. S. CODDINGTON,—

Dear Sir: On behalf of the officers and soldiers of this district, who desire to express, in some deliberate form, the deep grief with which the loss of their beloved President has filled their hearts, we respectfully invite you to deliver an Eulogy upon the deceased, at such time and place as will best suit your convenience.

We are, sir, very respectfully,
Your obedient servants,

(Signed)   JOHN P. HATCH,
Brigadier General Volunteers.

(Signed)   WM. GURNEY,
Col. 127th N. Y. Vols., Commanding City of Charleston.

(Signed)   JAMES C. BEECHER,
Col. 35th U. S. C. T., Commanding N. City District.

(Signed)   EDWARD H. LITTLE,
Maj. 127th N. Y. Vols., Commanding S. City District.

———

CHARLESTON, S. C., May 1, 1865.

To *General* JOHN P. HATCH,
Commanding Northern District, Department of the South;
Colonel WILLIAM GURNEY,
Commanding Post of Charleston, &c., &c.:

GENTLEMEN: Your letter of the 20th of April, inviting me, on behalf of the officers and soldiers of the Northern District of the Department of the South, to deliver an eulogy upon our lamented Chief Magistrate, ABRAHAM LINCOLN, has been received.

I know of no subject upon which human intelligence can be more justly and appropriately exercised than on portraying the virtues of that eminent victim of crime and venom.

I propose to carry out your wishes on Saturday, the 6th of May, as the earliest hour which my engagements will permit.

I have the honor to be, gentlemen,
Your very obedient servant,
DAVID S. CODDINGTON.

EULOGY.

———•———

SOLDIERS! who have saved the national life, why do I
stand here to-day the orator of desolation and death? Why
have ye half-masted that flag which now waves with new
meaning over our whole America?

Your arms are reversed, and yet there are no reverses;
your shields are craped in gloom, and yet the prospect is clear
and bright before us; no one dares to doubt your sublime
courage and heroic devotion, and yet you shrink here to-day,
unnerved and helpless, before the majesty of this bereave-
ment.

Alas! our national deliverer has fallen at the very gates of
the national deliverance. He who brought down the great
conspiracy to the dust is himself but dust. He at whose beck
a million of armed men moved upon the foe, had not one arm
to stay the cowardly trigger that swept him from the earth.

For four years crime and science sent forth their bulleted
thousands to crush or capture that life which a single finger
has reached and rended. Why could not the genius of disappointment capitulate gracefully? Why, when it had lost its
cause, did it not preserve its self-respect, and so descend to a
decent instead of a dastardly grave? Not that we would hold
an entire community responsible for prompting this deed, yet
the teachings of its leaders, the calumnies daily and hourly
heaped on that head toiling only for the public weal, acting
on a weak and insane temperament, produced their natural
fruits in this culminating crime. The purity of our Republican faith, the golden stream of our returning prosperity, has

been stirred and stained for the first time with the murdered life-blood of our first Citizen.

Just as we were sitting down to our second Union wedding feast, a skeleton stalks in upon the banquet.

Just as we had reached that bend in the river of Retribution, that angle of anxiety, where the implements of adjustment were succeeding the elements of destruction; just as the blood of contending armies was drying up and healing up on those silent and deserted battle-fields from which the South was limping away crushed and helpless, from whence the North was stalking forth strong and magnanimous, the demon of assassination soars to the very pinnacle of our triumph, treads the sacred summit of our civil system, enters with its grave venom the theatre of social recreation, where sits our great actor on the theatre of events; with stealthy step and ghastly cheek it leans over into the charmed circle amidst which power had forgotten everything but humor and friendship; its arm lifts—and our great and good friend vanishes forever. The chair of state sinks into the bier of death, on which lies the cold and clammy clod that was once the warm and useful life of ABRAHAM LINCOLN. Oh! who could have the heart to stop the beating of such a heart, whose every throb was for the glory and unity of our whole America? What brain could plan the dashing out of such a brain that so thoughtfully, so deeply, for years, had been planning our redemption? No quarter for him who never drew a drop of blood beyond the lines of war! No hope, no help for him who spared guilty thousands! On that day, all the pride of power, all the glory of victory, all the sense of superiority over foe and faction vanished. We heard not the tramp of our irresistible hosts, we saw not the glittering spears of our successful heroes as they moved in majesty over rebellion's prostrate and punished hordes, we saw nothing through our falling tears—nothing but a breathless martyr and an empty chair. Thousands had fallen to help victory; one, one death only could mar it, and that one nursed, cheered, led us up the mountain of our trial to leave us lonely and weeping at the peak.

Did the shallow soul who took this life, imagine that he could obstruct the current of ABRAHAM LINCOLN's cause by choking it up with ABRAHAM LINCOLN's corpse? Was he so ignorant of his victim's past as not to know that he who was to be injured was of all souls the most ready to forgive injuries? The South, which was to have been avenged by his death, was sure of more mercy, more help in their helplessness from this doomed man, than any unknown succeeding chief whom the exasperation of the North might precipitate in judgment upon the culprits. And even if the card sent by the assassin to the Vice-President had brought him within range of his shot, had the Speaker of the House, the President pro tem. of the Senate, the heads of departments all in their turn vanished from the official helm, there would have been so much merit to deplore, so many funerals to attend, but nothing else to miss or bury. No revolution to announce, no system to be swept away, whose roots are not in Washington, but in the hearts and habits of American citizenship. The constitution of the United States has worked its way into the constitution of every individual life. What is grounded in human nature, can only be eradicated by human nature. The habit and the influence of this republican system is so sure and so constant that the transition from one incumbent of office to another, is too natural, too necessary, to be disturbed by any violent displacement. For every LINCOLN dead, there is a LINCOLN to follow, without jar or disconcertion, beyond the sentiment and gossip of the hour. A LINCOLN, too, insisting on the same righteous conflict, the same redeeming policy; a policy reached and shaped thoughtfully, gradually, at first reluctantly, feeling its way timidly through the slow relaxing labyrinth of popular approval, until widely, almost unanimously, not by the freak or fanaticism of a man, nor in the hour of sure and exultant conquest, but proclaimed in suffering and in doubt, as the majestic resolve, the political and moral necessity, the deep self-convinced, self-defensive experience of a people determined not to come out of this fearful tempest with a right half yielded, a wrong half mended, and so a community wholly again insecure and vulnerable.

When a government depends upon an intelligent head, ruling an ignorant mass, the death of the one may be the upheaval of the other; but when the Chief of the State is but the type and the epitome of the average community, that whole community must die before the system perishes. Like most of the blunderers who have attempted to reason on the results of our war, the assassin underrated the republican system in educating the republican character. Calumny has erred more than it has benefited by reading history; because Rome split and Europe usually emerges from her great convulsions with old political lines obliterated, and a new construction of her civil relations, the great American Republic must degenerate into the same disruptions and divisions—forgetting that universal suffrage and universal knowledge were arches of salvation upon which no other republic had ever rested. A people who have the intelligence to see the right and the implement to secure it, are not born to meet the fate of nations who pass from commotion to commotion, with no interest and no voice in the result, because with no means to guide or influence it. "The great republic is gone," says the wise European philosophy of 1861. "Years of war, four or five republics, and then universal monarchy," exclaims the Count DeMorny. After the first six months, England was to interfere; then came another flash of prophecy; the military was to crush the civil power, a new Napoleon was to drive both houses of Congress out of the windows of the Capitol.

Thiers' *French Revolution* and Headley's *Napoleon and his Marshals* filled the weaker intelligence with these nightmares, as if soldiers, growing up and blooming all over with the blessings of such a government, possess the temptations to lawlessness of the French soldier, who knew nothing of the civil life of the past but by its oppressions; and who had acquired no discipline or experience of years to shape or steady whatever better policy he might think he was contending for. Then came the plausible financial prophecy—that the national purse could not stand the expense of the national safety—the difficulty was too vast, the outlay too enormous. No other people had ever met such a strain upon its resources without

bankruptcy. As if any other people ever possessed such
boundless resources to draw from, such floods of emigration,
such freedom from debt, such vast undeveloped treasure from
ocean to ocean, such awakened industry, and such universal
enterprise, which no nation in any hour of civil peace or civil
commotion could call upon to prop up its princes or its principles.

And now comes this most foul, fatal and depraved prophet,
who, more cruelly and terribly personal in the application of
his theory, imagines that if he can only strike down some of
the higher officers of the government, the confusion, the per-
turbation, the embarrassment that succeeds the blow may
topple down the principle and the structure of the government
itself; and so his dear South, lying helpless at the far end of
the plank, suddenly, by the weight of the fall, is lifted again
to rise and rule by anarchy if not by victory. Never before
has this stealthy state corrector—born of Mexican confusion
and European oppression—aimed its ghastly reform at America's
beneficent republicanism. The spirit of assassination is not
a reasoning spirit; if it had the mental energy to think, the
agitation of ideas would purify it. It is a senseless, nerveless,
mindless monster! too weak to argue, and too timid to
fight its victim; so it conceives its blow in meanness, and
strikes in darkness. Every assassin is a morbid egotist,
who, brooding on one idea, whether of revenge or reform,
reduces to a selfish personality the cause of his differences.
Great minds take their chances with great principles. If they
fail, the great man is appeased by the consciousness of right
or the martyrdom of failure. The little mind, with no vision
to comprehend either, substitutes nervous excitement for mental contemplation; and so, from love of notoriety or hatred of
those who differ with, or surpass him, becomes an assassin.
Calhoun could stab a nation with his logic, but how his nature
would have recoiled at such an enforcement. In the whole
history of assassination no striking man ever strikes the blow;
the obscure Brutus and his accomplices flow down to us only
on Cæsar's blood. Richard the Third threw on degraded roy-
alty no brighter gleam than flashed from his perpetually

descending blade. Ravillac, who murdered Henry of France, was a low, irresponsible fanatic. The murderer of the Duc de Berri, in depriving France of an amiable sovereign, blasted more on that day, than he had ever benefited in all his days. Russia's Peter and Russia's Paul and England's Perceval, all fell by men who never lifted themselves by word or deed above the little light that guided them to another's heart. And now, to-day, America's Lincoln comes down from a height loftier than his office, torn from the embrace of two millions of uplifting votes by the blow of a second-rate member of a second-class profession. The people who turned their backs on his acting have had to face his crime. He who knew nothing of government has succeeded in embarrassing it. He who spit upon the flag has half-masted it from Maine to California. The player who could not secure the attention of a single house has shook a continent and startled a century.

Yet when we remember how every life at all times is at the mercy of whatever insignificance or malignity chooses to assail it, we should thank the assassin for sparing Abraham Lincoln to us so long. A life that has passed through so many phases of public sentiment, so many important and momentous public actions, that life needed to be spared if it would be tested as the representative of the peculiar perils and novel trials of the American people—this life whose first official mission was to prove the right of the people to change their past peaceably in the orbit of the constitution; to renovate the old routine, to vindicate a new policy, to raise up and warm up more earnest men in the channels of public communication, to face anger without fearing or provoking it, to rebuke without wronging a community who had nothing to fear because no one to injure them. Let us thank the assassin for sparing him in that trembling interval between the ballot and the oath, between the 6th of November, 1860, and the 4th of March, 1861, when the elect of the people was permitted to take the people's chair before it was wrenched from him by the people's foe. Let us be grateful to the forbearing fiend for withholding his hand during that long range of eighteen months of mere defensive peace-beseeching war, when the innocent purposes of the President's election were so fully proved by the pertinacity with which he refused to disturb slavery. When that faithful hand, now cold in death, held on the rocking and reeling institution, through all the crimson sleet and blinding mist and fire of those murderous legions. and the lurid blaze from those incendiary ships which were shooting and burning out of the heart of the North all the forbearance which self-defense dictates to either policy or humanity.

Let us thank the wretch, too, for that further delay when the hour came for changing the government policy without changing its sense of duty; when the foe is to be punished more effectually by withholding the element that encourages his crime; when, having spared to the enemy more than he deserved, he could now concede to his friends all they asked; could help the fallen and the favored race, help the cause, the flag and the age, by one word, and that word, Emancipation. It was something to be permitted to pronounce it, to shut up a crime by opening our mouth, to break a chain as well as a conspiracy, to shoot this redeeming ray in the face of the thousands who died to stifle it, to throw such a light on this nation as no sun of genius or glory had ever shot along our American sky.

And now, after all the toil, the anguish, the doubt, the inexperience, the faith and the courage of four years of conscientious labor in unparalleled fields of statesmanship, it was something, too, to be permitted to go, with all his works, his fears and hopes, to the ballot-box, and from out its deep tones to hear that sweetest music in the ear of all candidacy, " Go forth, thou good and faithful servant, to a new lease of labor and glory." We thank our stars that this star was not quenched until the darkness which brooded over us had been scattered forever, crime punished, freedom safe, and the nation paramount. These were the aims of his policy and are the results of his efforts, and no bullet stepped between them and the crowning consummation of his life. They conclude his history, they round his eulogy, and they must crown his immortality. The scholar cannot read his annals and doubt that he was equal to the events which he administered, or that the events themselves were equaled by anything American since the advent of Washington.

If we look closely into the history of preceding administrations, we see how obviously connected was their line of policy growing out of the events that preceded them; how, in the unresisted exercise of its functions, the executive office is but comparatively plain sailing, despite of errors, and wranglings, and threats, which an appointment may modify, a message influence, or a veto arrest.

The nullification of South Carolina in 1833 never disturbed even a sheet of paper in the War Office or State Department. Most of our constitutional disputes, heretofore, have pointed to an increase or decrease in the powers to be exercised under that instrument; never to an extinction of its functions over any State or section. Since Shay's very trivial rebellion, not a pistol had been snapped in the face of the grand old charter.

No one administration since the adoption of the constitution has been confronted with any graver question than the charter of a bank, the reduction of a tariff, the status of a territory, the negotiation of a treaty, or the admission of a State, out of which logical convulsions often have arisen, but which the good sense of the people or the government have invariably adjusted. Mr. LINCOLN's administration was the most trying, because it found itself not with the measures of government disputed, but its very existence denied. With the oath over him to administer for all the States, he found State after State renouncing a jurisdiction he dare not release and could not control. In being peremptorily called on to accept the secession of States, he was invited to arrogate powers not granted to him in the instrument he was bound to support. Washington's term of office was a period of serious trial and anxiety to the friends of republican government. Nothing less than the influence of such a hero could have secured the successful adoption of a constitution with which so many wise men differed.

To secure a public opinion that would acquiesce in its jurisdiction, to reconcile the antagonism of leaders who distrusted each other's motives, and differed in their construction of the instrument they were aiding to administer, to substitute personal character and personal respect for tradition and experience, required a force of will, a delicacy of tact, an elevation of character, a superior confidence in the man which only such a hero could inspire. Popular intelligence in the time of our fathers would never have accepted this constitution from a conviction of its benefits. One party, fresh from the memory of British injustice, were for construing away all constraint on their actions; the other, more thoughtful, and fearful of the caprices of the multitude, insisted on approximating to the conservatism of monarchy. Washington, calmer and clearer than either, admonished them of both extremes, strenuously administering the government in a spirit of moderation and harmony that permanently secured us the beautiful system under which we have lived and prospered. The administration of John Adams involved no more important question than the necessity of relieving the nation of a Chief who had no faith in popular government. He was merely an eloquent, defiant electoral accident, a sort of intellectual isthmus between the harmonious grandeur of Washington and the great popular leadership of Thomas Jefferson. The presidency of Mr. Jefferson originated that democratic policy which for fifty years powerfully influenced the nation, and settled on a more comprehensive basis the influence of the people in public affairs—the grave of Federalism and the nursery of a new political organization, which, under different names, has preserved its distinctive national disorganizing features, ever since. Who now had the keener vision, Hamilton or Jefferson? In that storm of contending statesmanship, which almost shook the great chief from his chair, was it not Hamilton who prophesied that the Federal Government had most to fear from the encroachments of the States, and was it not Jefferson who, in his dread of central power, encouraged under the captivating and popular terms of "States Rights," "Federal Usurpation," all those little local laxitudes whose continuous buzz has so impeded for fifty years the music of the Union, and at last, through ambition and cunning, and the slow but sure unloosening of national ties by the intellectual training of the Southern young American in this plausible but perilous political school, brought us to this doubly perilous brink. Our real destiny, both political and geographical, begins with this administration. To it we are indebted for all that portion of our possessions included in the States of Louisiana, Arkansas, Kansas, and the Territories of Nebraska and Washington. It laid the basis of our future statesmanship, and with it many of our subsequent trials and dangers. James Madison succeeded to the legacy of English difficulties bequeathed to him by the preceding rule. Though a statesman of profound talents and amiable virtues, no man was ever more abused for timidity and inconsistency. One of the principal framers of the Constitution, he felt too deeply the responsibility that authorship involved not to act cautiously in any matter affecting its security. The issues presented during his administration—war with England and the assertion of our freedom on the sea as well as on the land—were of a nature rather to unite than divide the nation. It was in his time that the famous Hartford Convention met—the body to which Southern Secessionists proudly pointed as a proof that the Northern States had contemplated resorting to secession as well as themselves. Unfortunately for the argument, the Convention, which peaceably assembled, as peaceably dissolved, without resolving to raise even a finger against their best friend. If the North ever talk rebellion, they talk on till they talk themselves back to a more dutiful allegiance. In the administration of James Monroe, which is called by historians the era of good feeling, occurs the first warning of that terrible rending which slavery had in store for us. Yet the storm of the Missouri Compromise was quelled by a healthier public feeling than felled us. The succeeding President, John Quincy Adams, seated in the trough of the sea, between the wave of the Missouri difficulty and the billow of Nullification, moves on an easy swell to peace and oblivion. Then we come to the iron days of our inflexible Jackson, a soldier by feeling and profession, and no fiercer war on his hands than to hunt the Indian in a swamp, silence France with a demand for indemnity, South Carolina with a threat, and the great Bank with a veto. The succeeding regimé is but an elongation of this master influence, memorable for the secession of gold and silver from the currency, and a war of words over the burning *Caroline* as it plunged down the awful abyss of Niagara. With the advent of Tylerism, comes the second installment of ABRAHAM LINCOLN's future trials, in the annexation of Texas; then the election of Polk, with the sweeping down of the great and good men of both political parties; the war with Mexico; the coming in of golden lands, and the going out of the golden leaders who had kept up the health, the vigor and the integrity of the national sentiment. Later still, the Fillmore Administration advances with the Compromise of 1850—the last briefly successful struggle against the progressing arrogants of the slave power, when the dying giants of our land threw the weight of their names and nerves into the death struggle for peace and justice, expiring at the very threshold of their labors and leaving a helpless nation to drift on towards blinding darkness and blood.

With the Pierce Administration arrives the era of little men and great conspirators, of harmony disturbed and compacts broken, of fresh graves opened and jewels robbed from our illustrious dead.

In this administration the Republican party was born—in this administration was cut the timber from that Black Forest which was to kindle our recent unholy conflagration; and thus these master mischief-makers pile high the burden under which the later LINCOLN is to stagger. Soon the banner-blunderer, Buchanan, breaks on the lowering sky; around him gather all the ghastly gamesters for empire, who read their doom in the threatening minorities soon to rise to chastising majorities against their sacreligious plottings.

Here was woven the cotton shroud in which we have laid the dead South of the past—here was born in the Convention and vote of 1860 that pillar of fire for our night, that ABRAHAM LINCOLN whom this day we mourn and bless. This son of the prairie has found a high mountain range on which to rest his great and good deeds. We all remember the contest of 1860. In that crash of parties conscientious citizens hardly knew under which fragment to retreat with their bewildered opinions; whether to go rail-splitting at Chicago or hair-splitting at Charleston; whether to suffer respectable extinction with Bell and Everett, or to be frantically organized under the Southern Cross with Breckinridge and Lane.

The storm rose, the sun darkened, the earth reeled; on those heaving waves walked the trembling fortunes of America, demanding to be reassured by the exercise of a warmer fellowship and a more comprehensive patriotism. The Republican convention, too full of fear for favoritism, drops the giant of the Empire State and applies a more soothing sedative to the nervous commonwealth. ABRAHAM LINCOLN, though untried, was also uncursed; though unknown, for that very reason he could not be unpopular. And now who is this man they have caught up in a despairing tempest and lashed fast to this unsteady wheel? One indifferent Congressional term, one unsuccessful Senatorial contest are all the political capital he can drop into that anxious ballot-box. Yet they knew the stout character looming behind that lean reputation. They knew how much power a citizen may exhibit without the official exercise of power. How the open life of the press, the stump, and the tribune keep our American citizenship in constant communication with the men and the statesmanship of the times. How the active sympathies of the observing intellectual man broaden and deepen the range of his vision, and silently accumulate for him a fund of civil helpfulness always valuable and always liable to be called upon in great political emergencies. Born in Kentucky, a Southern State, reared in Illinois, a Northern State, he possessed just that graft which quickening with neither extreme would rule both in harmony. The sympathy of the South in feeling, the energy of the North in action, a pure life, a tested intellect, a varied experience identified with a new and growing community, who had earned by numbers, by patience, by population and power, a Presidential candidate; proved in general fidelity to party principles, yet unskilled in all partisan tactics and all vulgar partisan schemings; with none of those weaknesses so common to the most extraordinary men, without Webster's convivial excess, or Cicero's vanity, or Bacon's love of money, this spotless spirit rides the tempest, grinding no ax, but rebellion, to powder, and exhibiting no weakness but the lack of instant power to accomplish it. Where in the long line of our administrators will you find more real dignity of character with less assumption of it? While other Presidents economize their strength with official reserve and occasional seclusion from those incessant personal interviews which wear out the Presidential energies quite as much as more prominent exertion, Mr. Lincoln's sweep of good nature blew down all the fences around his position, and so left him out in common where the whole herd felt at liberty to browse. He was the first President who had time to see and hear every one. In civil war he has been civil to all. Blood never heated his blood. Place never made him forget his place. Thoughtful, studious, abstemious, industrious, the man of the people. Elected for all, with an ear for all, at home always in, his hand always out, ten chances to one if you or I go to the White House with a new invention to cradle wheat, a telegram from Gen. Grant's last battle does not surprise him with the instrument in his hand testing its merits in front of the White House. This is the democracy of manners linked to the democracy of principles. Sympathy for man which place cannot displace, and which springs only from the noblest natures, tested by the trials of the loftiest station. The war has produced nothing more remarkable than the growth of this character on the cause and the age. Our earlier Chiefs received the Presidency as the crowning official consummation of the people's gratitude for great and decisive services in their behalf. The later Presidents, from Polk to Buchanan, were men of moderate ability and of indifferent usefulness. Lucky creatures of availability, for party favors they performed a party's behests, imparting nothing to high station, but a warning against the principle that placed them there. Abraham Lincoln, born of the same principle of availability, the nominee and the elect of a mere party, the sins of that party to embarrass his administration of the cares and troubles of the country, an unknown man grappling with and groping through unknown dangers, many trembled for the vote they had given when they saw the huge black cloud charged with that extraordinary thunder lowering down on that seemingly ordinary creation of partisan manœuvreing. Some believed at first that the people had elected a joke to administer a calamity; that we had merely called on an awkward undertaker to lay out the cold remains of American liberty, so gracelessly did he seem to shuffle up to the temple of fame. Every man who found the President differing with his little way of settling our troubles, was sure we must go to ruin with such an ignorant pilot. Steadily and surely this perplexed chief toiled on through this mountain of misrepresentation; ever the result of capacity not yet proved, of plans not yet matured, of results not yet concluded, and a country still to be saved. How often, on winter nights, Heaven's borealian light has been mistaken for some distant barn-yard conflagration; how long, on our winter nights, we were in doubt whether our light upon a hill was but a rubbish blaze, to go out with the blast, or the sun that was to pierce the cloud and light us to redemption. Never had great power been wielded with such utter absence of egotism and self-sufficiency. Almost every administration has been a paraphrase of monarchical reserve in its communication and intercourse with the people. Now, in a moment of the greatest peril, when trouble provoked and provided for the power of a despot, ABRAHAM LINCOLN used authority with the sympathy of a friend, confronting crime in an odd and artless way, that pursued it with the restlessness of a fiend and punished it with the gentleness of a father. With what concise and plaintive music in his annual messages and occasional addresses he chants the misereres of our struggle, a model of new and sympathizing eloquence in statesmanship.

How anxiously and readily he turns to any source, however irresponsible, for any clue, however insignificant, that may lead to peace. How earnestly, at Niagara Falls, he plunges into the foaming question with "whomsoever it may concern," as to the terms upon which he will snatch them from the boiling abyss. How eagerly he explores the windings of the James and Appomattox for the lost jewel, taking the risk of seeming undignified rather than unyielding. Willingly he holds the guilty hand in his grasp if there is the slightest hope the dove may perch there. Thus, step by step, year by year, through trial, through contumely, ridicule, hatred, the scorn of a foreign and the target of a domestic foe, misapprehended even by friends, slowly, hopefully, certainly at last —the people see and the world acknowledges the great, good, peerless man that the convention of 1860 unwittingly stumbled upon. The calumniator is silenced, the battle is finished, the smoke lifts, and there stands our giant friend on the far height of our triumph, holding in one hand a captured South, and in the other the redeemed bondmen.

The grandest painting in all history, because proclaiming the grandest aim of all human effort, to baffle crime, which God abhors, and save freedom, which all men love.

Those who threw shells at this life now go trembling with flowers to his grave, calling on this departed spirit, this abused saviour, this Illinois ape, this tyrant, this hyena, to plead with that avenging "judgment," for this mercy their last great crime robbed them of. Who will say that the man who achieved these great results had not greatness in its best sense? The moral greatness of fortitude and purity of character, the mental greatness of wisdom to see farther, and eloquence to express better the duties and the relations of the hour, than any citizen, officially or otherwise, which cotemporary America could furnish. Does not this simplicity, this strength, this persevering earnestness, this hopeful, joyous, single-heartedness, this moral humility, this mental independence, this eloquence, too busy with the heart and the salvation of the hour to be subtle, ornate or elaborate, this cordial familiar miracle of work and humor, of faith and fear, of anxiety and energy, this eccentric dispenser of a most eccentric era, who will say that, with all his errors, his defects of insight and culture, this man was not miraculously meant to meet the precise exigencies of our calamity? Who will say that these high, broad American characteristics are not just the needs, with a little

2

more official experience, which make up the great comprehensive American necessities of our peculiar statesmanship?

ABRAHAM LINCOLN came into the world during the early part of this century. The compeer of Napoleon in power, he is also his cotemporary in birth. Though the same waters washed the jurisdiction of both, when born, how vast was the difference in their stations. Louis Napoleon was the favorite nephew of the mightiest conqueror of all ages. Born under the blaze of that eagle eye—announced to the world with glad salvos of artillery—rocked in the golden cradle of the luxurious Tuilleries, he knew nothing of the rude helplessness that struggled on the far frontier of unsettled America, amid rustic huts and howling wildernesses and Indian war whoops, whose cradle, if he had any, was rocked by the piercing blast that swept through the unsheltered domicile of an impoverished home. Behold now that dawning light beginning only with animal instincts and physical elements to aid its development. No gentle culture, no intellectual atmosphere, no chivalrous and traditional refinement to melt and mould its higher sentiment and deeper cravings. All those rules by which great men are systematically trained, by which Cicero and Fenelon, Fox and Burke, and our Webster, and even Clay, were unfolded and encouraged to advancing maturity, were denied him. Behold this granite will piercing these granite obstacles, through whose chinks gleam after gleam of helpful light is streaming until the stone crumbles, a broader flood descends, and the whole man, by self-culture and self-discipline, is lifted above the flatboat, above the rough right hand, into the higher brain, the loftier reach of legal knowledge, political power, and general usefulness. Slowly, step by step, he nears the far-off prince, whose birth is so hopelessly above his own. The one becomes a needy adventurer, an exile; the other is still an obscure attorney, but a man of local influence, who in dignity and self-respect would esteem himself equal to a seedy prince. Again they diverge far apart—convulsions shake the chronic storm-ridden home of the prince; the outlaw becomes France's necessity. The Bourbon's airy diadem vanishes—at his touch the uncle's imperial brilliant sparkles on the dull brow that brooded for years over its loss. The prince is the great Emperor of France, and a law to Europe's crowned imbecility. The obscure attorney grows apace. He has become the people's representative. Fortune, too, begins to light upon his lofty patience. By times the god descends, and the people in their princely capacity, passing by all the great lights who thought themselves born and reared, and who talked and twisted into all shapes, and bent their ears low and often to hear the sweet majestic sound that should call them to the Presidency, the people passing them all by, this humble, honest, direct, genuine man is dropped into that chair where Washington sat, and for which Webster sighed. And now these rulers born at the extremes of society, in France and America, face each other as peers. The one lifted by cunning, by nerve, and the help of a great name, to wear through blood the imperial purple of a fickle people. The other with the nobler arts of a noble nature, by wise service, by the advocacy of liberal sentiments, by abstinence from all sordid devices, comes up from the depths of the popular class to sway a vast empire, the equal of kings, with power and resources greater than France or England. Administering in peace the equal of several European kingdoms, and chastising with war a territory commensurate with half a continent. It may be that a severe criticism would exact a more familiar intercourse with governmental action, a deeper and more comprehensive reach of intellectual culture in the administration of important political interests; but when we consider the sagacity with which our great political and military struggle has been conducted, the easy grace with which intelligence by degrees counteracted inexperience, the vast amount of talent summoned to its assistance, the overflowing resources and the varied implements now awkwardly, now effectively, adjusting themselves to meet and master the monster wrong; the perfect simplicity, integrity and single-heartedness with which our lamented President's intercourse with the people has been signalized; how healthy his moral and personal tone has acted on the contest; with what perfect confidence his faith inspired our confidence; how familiarly and fatherly he has come down from the stilted formality of austere officiality to take our troubles by the hand; chucking them under the chin, and telling them to be of good cheer; mollifying the dangerous with appropriate and proper-turned touches of the humorous, using anecdotes as antidotes to keep human nature bland and cheerful under the constant pressure of the dreadful. This light-heartedness was not the levity of a frivolous indifference to grave duties, but a buoyancy born of a sanguine and genial enthusiasm, confiding in the success of the true and the good, and looking hopefully and gladly to pleasant results, through a consciousness of meaning and acting always for the interest of all.

No one suffered more intensely in these hours of doubt and gloom, when a triumph of the foe, on a battle field or at the ballot box, seemed to throw a momentary despair over the results of the contest. Here was a quiet citizen, faithful to every civil emergency, whose pure and persevering life, gifted with a terse and peculiar eloquence, disposed him to advocate his political doctrines with quaint and emphatic earnestness; this fresh and fearless man is suddenly called from an average routine of useful and responsible duties, to administer the complex machinery of the highest and most difficult trust of modern times. Who will ever forget that awful fall of 1860, when, amid the golden beauty of autumnal foliage, and the still more golden splendor of national peace and national power, we harvested the dark November ballot. It fell, the last calm flow of a nation's will through bloodless channels. It fell, that ghastly Presidential suffrage, amid the secret shudderings of a foreboding, yet still faithful, hopeful and peaceful Commonwealth. Bad men had promised to break up a good government if this good man succeeded to it. They had consented, voluntarily, to sit down and play the game, and when the LINCOLN ace turned up, attempted, like reckless blacklegs, to overthrow the table, and in the confusion snatch the stakes and enjoy the plunder.

Whence comes the philosophy of this dark suicide? Surely first in egotism. A people who hold another race in absolute subjection soon exaggerate their self-importance and believe all races their inferior. Because they could flog one people at will, they thought they had only to tie the North up by the heels and bring it to any terms. Northern Democrats could have no feeling of patriotism for their section when such august allies demanded submission. The next cause of their ruin was ignorance. Where was their arithmetic when South Carolina seceded? Who told them that one was greater than two; that the vast resources of the North would tremble before a Palmetto leaf; that the mud-sills could drive a bargain, but not an enemy; the shop-keeping crew might charge prices, but not batteries or bayonets? Had they forgotten or never read Revolutionary History? Was not the deep love of country drank in with our mother's milk, now tenaciously upheld with the red flow of our ready blood? Would the children of Warren and Putnam, of Schuyler and Greene, see this heritage swept away by the Davises and Lees of a more dastardly age?

Let those who are so proud of a separate South remember who gave them a South to be proud of. Who, when Marion was vanquished and Sumter and Lincoln swept from the contest, sent down our Greene and our hardy Northern help to lift their chain and restore their freedom and their fellowship with States, never for an hour knowing a country or a home distinct from the stronger and more protecting North. Thus they drifted on this frantic fraternity, with no light but phrensy and whisky, to their dark doom.

Public opinion was confused and bewildered by the senseless howl of State Sovereignty from this State bought for $17,500 by a company of English merchants. Look at the grievances alleged by the declaration of the South Carolina Convention. The North had all the ships and commerce, that was the crime of competition committed by their hard hands and honest labor. The North forced upon them a high tariff, and yet it was this South Carolina that insisted on a high tariff on cotton when we imported instead of exported that belligerent little fabric. The South had to help pay the $200,000 a year for fishing bounties to our seamen who sailed with their cotton and defended it on the high seas, while the North was paying their greater share of the million and a half of dollars it cost to carry the Southern mail, above its earnings. The North, in one or two States, refused to execute the Fugitive Slave Law, that is those States claimed the South Carolina privilege of nullifying an obnoxious Federal law, which the Federal Government faithfully fulfilled. These were the senseless arguments why the government of our fathers should be destroyed, why the whole fabric of organized society should be startled and loosened, why the nation should shake with the tramp of hostile brothers, why graves should be opened, homes desolated and hearts broken. Why ABRAHAM LINCOLN, an angel in feeling, and a Democrat in action, should be called by the Southern press and the Southern rulers a tyrant, a baboon, an ape, a lord over hyenas, and the sure prey of those giant reformers who were so skillfully and surely tracking him to his lair.

On the 4th of March, 1861, ABRAHAM LINCOLN swore to stand by the charter. He walked from the ballot-box to the inaugural over broken oaths and dissolving States. Under a Scotch cap he drifted by a threatening mob to find himself in the presence of a confounded people and a paralyzed government. Every aid was needed and no one could be trusted. Like the air, secession had insinuated itself into every crevice of public employment. Army and navy officers were resigning, and carrying off both experience and material. Clerks entrusted with the most important State secrets were sending them to the enemy, and if displaced the new might be equally as culpable. All enterprises were at a stand-still. Blood seemed the only business likely to thrive. Every one looked to him who had been accused of all this to remedy all this. There he stood, calm and anxious. A quiet man, who had come to perform a plain task, to execute laws which no one before had ever questioned, to satisfy the voters who had sent him there, and then leave it all as sacredly and securely safe, the rights of each and every section as he found them. Yet the storm howled on around this novice in statesmanship and in crime. More inroads on the holy temple, more whirling away of States, more faithful citizens renouncing their fidelity to a common mother. The contest deepens. Brothers are sharpening for their brother's blood. Statesmen who could easily solve ordinary questions, shake their heads at the shaking fabric. Public sentiment is divided as to the powers of a government founded on sentiment. Can you punish the author and the owner for what they do with their own? Has not a Sovereign a right to its sovereignty? Thus was the nation bewildered, staggered, lowered, and drunk with the sophistry of Southern phrases, until one day a lunatic in Montgomery telegraphed to another demented to fire on that sacred bunting. The ball comes on and knocks the film from our drowsy Northern eyes, lifts the clouds that had obscured our self-defence, and we rise to the height of both our danger and our duty. Before Sumter all was party. Not the nation, but how should the Republicans act. Would concessions be consistent with the rights and results of a party victory? How dare defeat bully us. Sumter's ball hurled ABRAHAM LINCOLN from the Chicago Platform to the Springfield Armory. It made every American citizen an office seeker, asking a place for his country among the nations; asking for his own plundered citizenship; every man was a government contractor that day, pleading for the Great Contract. Now ABRAHAM LINCOLN is himself; now he puts on his official pea-jacket, goes on the national deck, and grasps the helm with that dauntless vigor which God and his Western life had given him. This bullet of Sumter relieves him of all that civil diffidence to which an unpracticed prominence is prone and which even paralyzed the experience that preceded him. With more necessity of blood comes more desertion of States. All who stand by the stability of national power need this crumbling away of the yielding, unreliable material which might impede or fraternize indifferently with the supreme exigency; and now the question is, Who shall awake and lead the military element. All our hope of glory and soldierly experience is centered in one tottering, fading, faithful giant. Scott of the past must be succeeded by some younger Scott. With a childish enthusiasm the people adopt and exult over an unknown youth, modest and cultivated. With the generosity of unaccustomed war they gorge this untried hero with powder, and

ball, and men, and confidence, and every implement of success,
that could make merit succeed and the lack of it snarl and
fall.

Through all that period of criminal caution and incompe-
tency, how nobly the faithful President stood by him whom
an intelligent impatience was demanding to be removed. How
anxiously his kind nature sustained this wooden hero, and
urged him from splendid retreat to splendid retreat, to prove
himself at last all this hopeful people hoped of him. With
what eager pertinacity his disappointment turned from chief
to chief, searching under every repulse for the true leader;
poring over that bloody volume of the War Directory to find
the name and residence of him who was to lead this nation to
victory and unity.

During the first two years of the war, our greatest general
was our general greatness. Alternately checked and chasing
the elastic foe on innumerable battle-fields, yet still advancing,
at last from fire-vomiting impediments, wide-spread toil and
slaughter, are evolved in smoke and blood, as the genii by the
sea rose out of storm and mist, so rose our Grant, Sherman
and Farragut, to lead back through fields of ceaseless triumph
the reeling, staggering spirit of Union and Liberty. These
are the names that make our cause strong, and would make
any cause dangerous. We know, too, whose clear eye first
discovered their merits, and whose hand signed the instru-
ments that sent them forth to hew away all obstacles that
stopped *E pluribus unum's* path from the Lakes to the Gulf.

This unknown man, a stranger to office and statesmanship,
to public praise or public blame, without great genius or great
experience, or great fame, acquired or traditional, to gild error
or confirm merit; with a name to make, an oath to keep, a
people to save, a crime to punish, the volcano heaving under
his feet, the oath warning him over his head, the dagger at
his breast, an empire in his hands, backed by a divided North,
defied by a seemingly united South, his obscure and spotless
name at once the synonym of England's sneer and Richmond's
curse; with only a pure heart, a clear eye and a steady hand
to lay without flinching on the most dangerous crisis, the

most doubtful issues, the most perplexing duties, the most daring and defiant, the most well-bred, well-considered, comprehensive, cultivated, hell-engendered plot that ever dashed its bloody hand and icy heart against the elements of law and order. He found himself heir to a statesmanship confused, shuffling and pusillanimous, occupied only with the question as to how we should permit our institutions to be murdered most gracefully, and he left its public policy candid, earnest, self-sustaining, engaged only with the question how the attempted murderers could be treated most mercifully. He found American nationality suddenly confronting him as a disgraceful doubt; he parted with it a terribly-respected fact. He found the government a dissolving giant, dying of an old cancer that had baffled the best physicians; he lived to cut out the poison with his sword, and find his well-knit, well-mannered, vigorous, compact patient a perpetual and healthful mourner at his grave. Sorely in need of force to meet the arming crime, he found our little navy had been sent yachting in the Indian and Pacific Seas, that treason might cruise more seriously along the streams of our progress. He lived to fill the world with our swarming ships, original in design, invincible in defense, terrible in destruction, able to defend one continent and defy another. He came into possession of 15,000 regular soldiers, scattered over as many miles, and 1,000,000 of men by him equipped reversed their arms on his funeral march. He found the people quailing under a debt of eighty millions and fearing the weight of it must bar the door to national salvation; he left them with their country redeemed, their resources more developed, their trade increased, and a mountain of three thousand millions of debt scaled at all points for investment, without officially calling on a single foreign dollar to help us purchase our domestic safety. He found the public feeling and the sense of citizenship demoralized, the tone of political responsibility lowered, the suffrage a mere vehicle for partisan aggrandizement, the love of country at the mercy of a States' right dogma, a party tie, a demagogue's breath; national obligations, confused and evaporating in a narrow local selfishness that would part with an empire to save a hobby, that would not give up a prejudice to keep up the wisest and most beneficent systems ever sworn to by man. He lived to see the sun dawn on a united people purified by suffering ; their sense of danger elevating their sense of duty and unity. By personal example of earnest, disinterested public service, by patience, courage and faith in all well-doing, more than by sermon, homily or proclamation, did this good chieftain mould the better life of the nation and preserve it from false prophets and false issues ; keeping it in the steady line of calm and inflexible determination to pass through its perils, to accept its sacrifices, to live up to its duties, and so save all that heroism had acquired and freedom and virtue sanctified. He accomplished all this, not without, perhaps, many errors of inexperience and defects of judgment : not without sometimes ringing the little bell a little too often, or drawing the bolt a little too soon ; sometimes overworking the war power, in which fewer mistakes could hardly have been made with so many crimes to lock up and use up ; the people preferring the occasional despotism of mistakes to the permanent despotism of crimes—preferring an incompetent man, sometimes inadvertently kept in office, to an absurd cause enthroned forever. He passed through this storm of war, this criticism of civil duty, these murmurs of complaint, these periods of panic, to victory and immortality, not without much help from heaven, many friends, brilliant aids and immense resources. He saw a foreign oligarchy envious and malignant, banded to write down and wear down the purest and most powerful type of modern republicanism ; he saw a home opposition, reckless, wanton and depraved, showering his most righteous acts with defiant slanders and cruel perversions in a crisis entitled to magnanimity and a generous forbearance ; he saw this dastardly tribe brought down, humbled and helpless, before the simple efforts of persistent and well-directed achievements ; he saw the South that had exhausted upon him every epithet and every feeling of hatred and calumny, who had taught their slaves to ridicule him, their children to loathe and lisp the alphabet of never-ending scorn and bitterness, he saw this South staggering and dying under his incessant blows, lifting its fainting head to deny and to regret a death which might uncomfortably precipitate them from the chastisement of principle to the chastisement of revenge.

To all these merits of energy, patience, probity, sagacity, eloquence, and aptitude for organization and execution, which distinguished the great emancipator, must now be added the melancholy merit of national martyrdom. As in his life his achievements render his rule the most important and conspicuous Presidential career since Washington's, so in his death he stands alone as the first public character violently swept from the sphere of its usefulness; a great guardian stricken down from the side of a great truth, just as it was passing from the perils of war to the exigencies of peace. Will not emancipation—this infant, born in the hail of blood-blinding war—will it not miss that relaxed hand, that stilled voice, as the orphan totters through opposing ranks to rank and power?

Abraham Lincoln fell on the very day the old flag came down on Sumter; when we stood on that ruin which was yet more the ruin of the South; but not till his soul had gone up with the flag; not until the pertinacity of the North had waved a mended principle over a broken fortress. And now, with this loved one vanished, this Union saved, this sad Southern people prostrate, this peace perched on every surly battlement of rebellion, will the South pass thus sullenly from the eminence of defiance to the extreme of apathy and indifference?

Why is it that in all these conquered districts we hear so much of the people's love of the Union, and no attempt to work up this Union feeling into State organization and national co-operation? All ready to cringe to power, to forswear the past, ready to take rations, take oaths, take office, take anything to save property and avoid the last ditch. Where is all that manhood which braved death, defied the world, and staked everything for Jeff.? That rebelled, robbed, lied, slaughtered, hung, and burned for the right to break up, and will do nothing to make up, that involves reason, thought, loyalty, and earnest political brotherhood.

Come back, oh deluded and defeated South. Come back

in feeling as you are already back by compulsion. Those who won you with their superior sword would hold you by the equal charter. For blows and curses, for hard names and light fingers, for ruin diverted from abroad and baffled at home, for all but the leadership in your hellish crimes, we offer just laws, equal rights, and a common share in that loving government only made more immortal by warding off the death-blow you would have dealt it.

With all the desolation of your fields and homes, you have lost nothing permanently but a traitorous crew and a poisonous creed; nothing which industry will not repair and patriotism secure. Remember, slavery was never in danger until you lost your senses; remember, too, that it never can be restored until we lose ours. The same talent and energy employed in the arts of peace that you have exhibited in war, the same toil with your white hands, the same endurance of fatigue and hardships, of hunger and danger, through desperate encounters and dreary marches which made you the slaves of slavery, by peaceful free labor, will restore you to a nobler and more abundant prosperity than was ever wrung from the toil of others. You can hire the negro's freedom cheaper than you can buy his servitude. The interest on his slave value will almost pay his free wages, while his own interest in the rights of men will increase the energy with which he develops your wealth. Free labor alone has conquered you. It invites emigration, it develops and then accumulates resources too vastly and too quickly for slavery to compete with. The negro, as slave, failed to keep off war or to keep up war for your advantage, now try if the negro as freeman, may not prolong peace and so insure harmony, unity, and a less sensitive form of progress and prosperity. Will you forget that you must arouse, organize, and recover your lost civil status? As war has thrashed out of you the beaten and demolished theory that a State may defy and destroy a nation, why not heartily and permanently shape the State law and conform every local obligation and every moral and political sentiment to the spirit of national duty; co-operating in cheerful concurrence with the great Federal amendment, so that never directly or by implication shall any clause be so doubtful in the constitution as to tempt the traitor or wean the patriot from fealty to the supreme law of the Union, and thus divert misery and ruin from yourself and your children to the latest generation.

Will not this Southern people call conventions, appoint elections, send delegates back voluntarily to that Congress they voluntarily spurned, and thus, in the good American way, by argument, by peaceful investigation and hopeful reference to representative and judicial adjudication, submit their rights and wants, under a returning submission and sense of duty, to those who in their better days decided wisely and well for us all; or else, in stubbornness and anger, remain under this military post-garrison form of pupilage, or go forth wanderers to people some more Southern solitude; or, like the Arab or the gipsy, intrude on luckier races branded with the marks of unrespected martyrdom. Laws, habits, language, feeling, kinred, make us one people. Love and trade, as well as mountains and rivers, matrimony, as well as geography, have made us one people. You cannot form two nations of a community with a Yankee aunt and grandmother hanging up reverently in every Southern parlor, with a Southern sister or grandfather piously packed away in every Northern home. Is the Southern pride wounded by defeat? The very exertions that have been vanquished have made them famous, and by the industry of the effort prepared them for that free labor which they could not avoid. If they have lost their slaves they have gained themselves—gained knowledge, gained self-reliance, and a surer and quicker development. Admitting that the whole value of the slaves was one thousand millions of dollars, which they have lost, yet it is not one-half the sum the North has had to pay to maintain the Government. Are they desolate and impoverished? Not more so than any desperate speculator who embarks his all in some such wild-cat bank and fails. If they *will* invest in damnation, they must expect their profits to be hell. If the negro proves himself worthy of free labor it will ensure to Southern ambition more political power by enlarging the Southern constituency; it will make Southern lands more valuable by increasing their productiveness; and with the generous tender of Northern capital, this Southern community must rapidly recover from its depletion.

And now, soldiers! sons of our North! saviours of our nation! your days of danger and strife are drawing to a close. No heroes of the world tread more enviable heights of fame. Your bayonets have been gleaming spires over that holy church of liberty in which your fathers and your brothers worshipped.

Through all your marches you have never forgotten that you were citizens as well as soldiers; that you were moving at no unrighteous conqueror's beck. Amid all the storm of battle, on picket, through the drill, or by the camp fire, the spirit of your Government was simply calling upon you to perfect your own citizenship. No cannon could drown that voice—no raid capture the resolution to obey it.

The glory of your deeds will remain with you through life; it will influence your character and insure you respect. The sight of that old flag when it flits between your cares and your dreams and waves over some civil duty abandoned on holidays or festivals, you will think how you followed it as it streamed on fields of fire. How the nation reeled or righted as you shrunk from or breasted the guilty lines that confronted it.

And as your eyes gleam with exultation over the dangers you escaped, and the rights you snatched from the traitors' grasp, you will mingle your glad refrain with loved memories of that great and good chief who first called you into service, equipped you for battle, and with a father's care and a monarch's power, followed you with cheering words through every contest, until the bullet that spared you laid low his life, fresh from the freedom of one race and the safety of another.